RIPPLES

A Book of
Spiritual
Pause and Ponder

James B. Harshfield

RIPPLES
A Book of Spiritual Pause and Ponder

All Rights Reserved 2002 by James B. Harshfield

No part of this book may be reproduced or transmitted
in any form or by any media, graphic, electronic, or
mechanical, including photocopying, recording, taping,
or by any information storage retrieval system, without
the permission in writing from the publisher.
Printed in Korea

First Printing: Copyright by James B. Harshfield 2000
                    Published by iUniverse

Second Printing: Copyright by James B. Harshfield 2002
                    Published by Rockjack Books
                    P.O. Box 170268
                    Boise, Idaho 83717-0268

Art Work: Mary Blackeye, Petoskey, Michigan 49770
                    Email: blkeye@racc2000.com

Book Design: Mark Kashino, Kashino Design
                    PO Box 27, Hailey, Idaho 83333
                    Website: kashino.com

Library of Congress
Control Number: 2002092692

ISBN 0-9719567-0-7
US $18.95

Acknowledgements

I extend a special thanks to Mark, Hugh, Jo Ann, Bob, Charlene, Steven, Larry, Janet, Ann, and Barb for their assistance with this book.

The special talents of Mary Blackeye created the artwork.

A special thanks to Gloria Carlson for the extra time and effort she devoted to editing the pages of Ripples.

Dedication

Family is a power that reaches from the past, finds meaning today and extends hope for a better tomorrow. Therefore, I dedicate this book to Mom and Dad, Larry, John, Angela, Bev, Fred and in memory of Helen and Walter.

Preface

Ripple's is a collection of meditations and short studies offered for the consideration of the reader. The purpose is not to convince or prove, but rather to cast the concepts upon the pond of the reader's mind. Perhaps a unique response will create a "Ripple" outward as the ideas grow within.

James Harshfield

Contents

Acknowledgements iii
Dedication v
Preface vii
Introduction xi
Life 1
    Meditation on Life and Death 3
    Now 4
    The Door 5
    Worldly Gods 6
    Stepping Forth 7
    Choices 8
    Ripples of Life 9
    In Oneness 10
    Seasons of Life 11
    The Conflict 12
    Words of Wisdom 13
    Symptoms of a Weakness 14
    Freedom 15
    The Sequence Part 1: The Way 17
    The Sequence Part 2: The Resistance to Change 18
    The Sequence Part 3: The Solution 19
    Have You Met Grace? 20
    Ripples of Life 21
Love 23
    Meditation on Love 25
    Pause and Ponder 26
    Words Alone 27
    Laws or Love 28
    Love 29
    Sin 30
    Bridges 31
    The Rose 33
    The Whisper 34
    Words of Wisdom 35
    Marriage 36
    It is Good to Know 37
    Love Is 38
    Ripples of Love 39

- Sacrifice ... 41
  - Meditation on Sacrifice ... 43
  - Humility ... 44
  - Give Thanks ... 45
  - Suffering ... 46
  - How Is It Done ... 47
  - The Mind ... 49
  - Eternal Truth ... 50
  - Suffering ... 51
  - The Song ... 52
  - Humility ... 53
  - The Song of Source ... 54
  - Ripples of Sacrifice ... 55
- Virtue ... 57
  - Meditation on Virtue ... 59
  - We, the Gathering ... 60
  - Mystery ... 61
  - Ripples of Virtue ... 62
  - The Inheritance ... 63
  - Give to Me ... 64
  - The Cup of Wisdom ... 65
  - Beyond The Veil of Time ... 67
  - Lasting Satisfaction ... 68
  - Faith ... 69
  - Doing The Word ... 70
  - A Flowering Heart ... 71
  - Pass It On ... 72
  - Ripples of Virtue ... 73
- Wisdom ... 75
  - Meditation on Wisdom ... 77
  - Let's Get Focused ... 78
  - Ripples of Wisdom ... 79
  - It is Good to Know ... 80
  - Images in Contrast ... 81
  - Mercy and Justice ... 82
  - Boldness without Kindness ... 84
  - The Balancing Act ... 85
  - Reality ... 86
  - The Mountain ... 87
  - Ripples of Wisdom ... 89
- The Author ... 90

Introduction

Ripples: A Book of Spiritual Pause and Ponder is a carefully written collection of verses dedicated to spiritual enrichment. The direct, short freestyle verses allow the reader to freely interpret the text on an individual basis through the guidance of the Spirit of Truth. The thought provoking images help open the mind and soul to the beauty of God in the world. The diverse spiritual ideas merge together to make a beautiful collage of love, hope, faith and peace. The calming effects of the words can warm the heart and caress the soul.

LIFE

Meditation on Life and Death

"I have set before you life and death,
the blessing and the curse.
Choose life, then, that you and your
descendants may live by
loving the Lord, your God,
heeding His Voice,
and holding fast to Him."

Deuteronomy 30:15,19

Now

It is in the now we grasp the flow of life.

It is in the now we
> hear the music,
> smell the flowers,
> see the beauty around us,
> feel the warmth of a loving touch,
> savor the delicious tastes of our tables.

It is now we can
> say a prayer,
> experience joy,
> share in love.

Only now is the Divine Presence found.

The Door

Our Father provides:

the door;	but we must	open it.
the truth;	but we must	accept it.
the faith;	but we must	believe.
the trust;	but we must	endure.
the peace;	but we must	hope.
the dignity;	but we must	respect.
the guidance;	but we must	surrender.
the mercy;	but we must	forgive.
the blessing;	but we must	give thanks.

Our Father provides the way and the understanding,
    but
        we must choose,
        we must act,
        we must submit.

Worldly Gods

Have we chosen worldly gods?
Have we become entrapped in a hamster wheel,
an endless cycle of seek and attain,
seek and attain?

What have we allowed to control our daily lives?
Have we become entrapped in a hamster wheel,
an endless cycle of seek and attain,
seek and attain?

How are we spending our time and effort?
Have we become entrapped in a hamster wheel,
an endless cycle of seek and attain,
seek and attain?

Is our goal self-satisfaction, self-gratification?
Have we become entrapped in a hamster wheel,
an endless cycle of seek and attain,
seek and attain?

Maybe it is time to choose again.

Stepping Forth

We are invited to escape the enticing power of this world.
To achieve this goal,
> we must be willing to step forth in faith
> and discover the hidden mystery of divine love.

Human nature resists this journey into the unknown.
Our companions on this trek
> may be fear, doubt and uncertainty.

Yet, if we stay the course in trust,
> the door into divine power will open in our lives.

Choices

Live to spread peace
>	or to harbor anger.

Live to bring harmony
>	or to be resentful.

Live to offer forgiveness
>	or to seek vengeance.

Live in joyfulness
>	or grope in bitterness.

Live in love
>	or struggle in self-pity.

Live in divine trust
>	or abide in doubt and confusion.

Ripples of Life

As the artist produces a beautiful work of art,
so
the Father fashions each person
into
a special creation.

God moves in the halls of kings
and
rests in the homes of the poor.

People make history,
but
God makes history reflect divine purpose.

God walks in the alleys of the world
and
swims in the sea of humanity.

In Oneness

God is the Star…
    We are the Twinkle.

God is the Sun…
    We are the Light.

God is the Earth…
    We are the Grass.

God is the Sky…
    We are the Birds.

God is the River…
    We are the Fish.

God is the Food…
    We are the Hunger.

God is the Song…
    We are the Voices.

God is the Melody…
    We are the Dancers.

Seasons of Life

A summer of faith may be followed
by
a fall of doubt.

A winter of testing may be followed
by
a spring shower of blessings.

The Conflict

It is not easy to place trust in the unseen God.
Our consciousness resists trusting in an unknown nature.

Our minds are most comfortable with information that is
 substantiated by our five senses.

Oftentimes, when we choose to depend on the unseen Father,
 we experience uncertainty, fear, and distrust.

The Prize is gained and understanding grows
 when we move beyond the act of choosing
 and into the heart of eternal trust.

Words of Wisdom

Fear and doubt
are
symptoms.

Great suffering enters the world
through
the worship of worldly treasures.

Love of money and possessions
can be
the short chain to eternal enslavement.

Envy of other people
feeds
the insatiable appetite for more.

Symptoms of a Weakness

Sensing limited satisfaction.
Sensing limited security.
Sensing limited peace and happiness.

    Experiencing constant strife.
    Experiencing constant struggle.
    Experiencing constant self-doubt.

      Feeling inadequate.
      Feeling unfulfilled.
      Feeling fear and doubt.

Controlled by the constant desire for more possessions.
Controlled by anger, hate and envy.
Controlled by the craving for more power.

Freedom

Freedom
comes from escaping the snares
of
desire and craving.

We are called to live in the present moment
where
we can truly experience
God's forgiveness and understanding.

By placing ourselves in the hands of Divine Providence:
we reject doubt and fear,
we live in hope and trust,
we practice love and faith,
we pledge our acceptance to whatever may come.
Only then are we finally free.

The Sequence
Part 1

My Way

We will ultimately experience frustration and failure when we are dominated by:

striving	for	more sensual satisfaction;
focusing	on	gaining more and more possessions;
desiring	to	control and dominate;
striving	for	constant rewards and achievements;
depending	on	logic and season to make decision;
craving	for	immediate rewards and fulfillment.

The Sequence
Part 2

The Resistance to Change

The following are reasons for not yielding to the Word of Truth:

fear of the unknown;

fear of being hurt;

fear of losing control;

fear of being humbled;

fear of rejection;

fear of failure;

fear of change.

The Sequence
Part 3

The Solution

The following are ways to embrace a life of goodness:

responding	to	the call of faith;
submitting	to	a life governed by love;
yielding	to	a trust beyond reason/logic;
ceasing	to	go it alone;
admitting	to	the power of forgiveness, both given and received;
surrendering	to	Divine Wisdom.

Have You Met Grace?

I would rather have done it myself. Why should I place my trust in the hands of another? I was strong, determined and intelligent. I had the power to find my own solutions. So, I sat, working at the task of being successful for many years.

I placed the incomplete puzzle on the table of life. I arranged the pieces into a pattern of conquest. I knew I could ultimately gain control.

There was a knock at the door. I told the caller to go away. I kept striving to satisfy my unlimited craving. I worked to gain more things and be more involved; yet, I found my emptiness growing. I was lonely and frustrated; I found limited enjoyment and fulfillment in life.

There came another knock at the door. Out of curiosity and boredom, I decided to open it. The warmth of a gentle Light embraced me. I heard the words, "Follow me. Through steps of faith you will find the answers for all you need to know and understand. Complete the circle so that your puzzle of life may be completed."

I feel comfortable following my new, simple path of life. After the lonely days of self, it is a special gift to live in trust, peace and harmony. Personal problems still come, but I find hope in the gentle presence of Grace.

It has been many days since I decided to live within the beauty and challenge of Grace. Grace provided the power to escape the bondage of selfish behaviors. I found that my response to Grace is a full circle. I know that we are called to complete the circle by returning Light as Light and offering Love in response to Love.

Ripples of Life

The warmth of caring acts
can melt an icy heart.

We are to be a hand-on-the-shoulder
to each other.

Truth strolls in the garden of the human spirit
and
waits to be invited into the home of human awareness.

Heaven does not take applications;
your resume is already on file.

In the end,
it will be a conversation between you and God.

LOVE

Meditation on Love

"God is Love. He who abides in love, abides in God and God in him."

1 John 4:16

Pause and Ponder

Love speaks through its presence.

To act in love
is
to share
in the presence of Divine Wisdom.

Listening opens the mind to the Word of Truth.
Listening offers the gift of respect.

Love is not just
now;
love is eternal.

Words Alone

Words alone do not create the climate
      for our movement
           into the heart of eternal goodness.

Words and ideas
         can help direct the reasoning mind.

Yet, the door into the spiritual life
         is gained through Love.

As we express love,
         we experience the fabric of the universe
         and the essence of existence.

Laws or Love

laws judge, and love forgives;

laws condemn, and love heals;

laws close, and love opens;

laws maintain, and love multiplies;

laws define, and love understands;

laws limit, and love creates;

laws bind, and love frees;

laws dictate, and love guides;

laws institute, and love fashions.

Love

Love does not make haste,
    but waits in patience.

Love is not rigid,
    but moves gracefully in life.

Love does not enslave,
    but lives in freedom.

Love does not manipulate,
    but encourages growth.

Love does not act alone,
    but finds presence among people.

Sin

Sin   creates   barriers.

Sin   is   a choice.

Sin   seeks   only self.

Sin   defiles   community.

Sin   can   last forever;

unless,

Love builds bridges.

Bridges

Love builds bridges.

A network of goodness supports these bridges, allowing
them to span improbable distances
between people.

Love builds bridges.

The Rose

Images of love are found in the Rose:

    in the promise   of   the bud;

    in the beauty   of   the opening petals;

    in the fragrance   of   the essence;

    in the peace   of   the garden;

    in the demands   of   the thorns;

    in the gift   of   its life pressed and held in remembrance.

The Whisper

The Whisper reaches forth into the dimensions of time and space.
The Whisper
  pierces eternal domains,
  touches each moment,
  caresses the essence of existence.

The Whisper
  is alive within the throb of nature
  and it can be heard
  beneath the roar of the human consciousness.

The Whisper flows from the very origin of life.

The Whisper speaks softly to each of us.
The Whisper is an invitation to complete the eternal quest.

We can respond to the Whisper,
  by following the guiding power of creation within us.

This trek is an adventure into the mystery of the Whisper.
This journey shapes our existence
  into a unique expression of love.

A love that is both an example and a promise
  to people we meet along the journey of life.

Words of Wisdom

Inner peace
is
greater than anything we can possess in this world.

Outside appearances
do not always
tell the inside story.

Political and personal powers
offer empty promises
in a world needing eternal solutions.

Some days there
seem to be
more
challenges than faith.

Marriage

A commitment to love leads from:

me	to	us,
mine	to	ours,
taking	to	giving,
neglecting	to	caring,
talking	to	listening,
ignoring	to	supporting.

It Is Good To Know

God is never
        neutral,
        passive,
        uninvolved.

God
is
found in each moment of now.

God is
        intimate,
        caring,
        compassionate,
        involved,
        forgiving.

Love Is

Love	is	a universal summons to all people.
Love	is	a decision.
Love	is	an action.
Love	is	a living prayer.
Love	is	the perfect response to love.

Ripples of Love

Love gathers; sin separates.

Love,
to be known
must be experienced.

Love and forgiveness
are
the doors to spiritual healing.

If we are not an example of love,
then
we are a distraction.

SACRAFICE

Meditation on Sacrifice

"For in sacrifice you take not delight,
burnt offering from me you would refuse;
my sacrifice, a contrite spirit,
a humbled contrite heart,
you will not spurn.

Psalm 51:18-19

Humility

Humility grows from the recognition of human frailty.

The roots of vanity
can be removed
by
humility.

Humility knows the weakness of conceit.

Humility
acknowledges
the power of modesty.

Humility helps us accept
what
we cannot change.

Give Thanks

Give thanks when people ignore you,
    and learn to appreciate a friend.

Give thanks when people lie to you,
    and learn to trust in God.

Give thanks when people steal from you,
    and learn the fleeting values
    of material things.

Give thanks when people hurt you,
    and learn the value of suffering.

Give thanks when people manipulate you,
    and learn the meaning of forgiveness.

Suffering

The natural forces of life
(not the Father)
create the potential for suffering.

Fear
pain
doubt
anger
despair
craving
rejection
are agents of suffering.

Suffering
grows from the pain
of
body, mind and spirit.

Suffering exposes our human frailty.

Suffering reveals
our need for the healing touch
of the
Divine Physician.

The agony of suffering reveals our need for God.

How is it Done?

By Creation   we   have Potential.

By Faith   we   receive Grace.

By Acceptance   we   empower Change.

By Belief   we   know Truth.

By Trust   we   gain Peace.

By Surrender   we   attain Freedom.

By Love   we   live in Wisdom.

By Forgiving   we   are Forgiven.

By Prayer   we   find Wholeness.

The Mind

The ability to control our thoughts is necessary
before spiritual growth is possible.

The power of the mind
can create barriers or open doors.

A habit of thinking can be difficult to change;
the mind clings to old memories
and old ways.

The way we
view ourselves and interpret the events of life
create and reinforce
patterns of behavior.

Self-discipline is essential to challenge
the tyranny of the mind
which desires control over the spirit.

Eternal Truth

Turn to Eternal Truth for guidance;
        forget the vain examples of selfishness.

Turn to Eternal Truth for support;
        forget the toys of this world.

Turn to Eternal Truth for love;
        forget the behaviors of conceit.

Turn to Eternal Truth for comfort;
        forget the empty pleasures of greed.

Turn to Eternal Truth for wisdom;
        forget the desire for personal power.

Suffering

Suffering can open doors to
hope,
peace,
wisdom.

Suffering can live in harmony
with
love and joy.

The essence of suffering
is
difficult
to understand and to accept.

Divine Wisdom can offer meaning
to the
most painful situations.

Suffering does not redeem.
It purifies.

We are invited to drink of the Cup of Wisdom.

The Song

The light of a new day grew into a faint and mysterious Song. The dawn's brilliant colors and soft hues blended into a provocative harmony. The Song wove a pattern of indescribable beauty. The beckoning call of the music was transformed into a simple rhythm with a lasting melody whose message was optimism.

My excitement was growing with a widening sense of hope. So often I had pursued the alluring trinkets of this world, and they had melted into empty satisfactions. Yesterday's selfish accomplishments had created doubt and emptiness. Now, my acceptance of the Song could be the beginning of a new life.

Yesterday, my accomplishments in life seemed insignificant and void; I was losing my sense of validity. Oh how I had longed to escape the dark blanket that engulfed my soul with despair! Now, with the promise of the Song, my yesterdays could be transformed by the guidance of Eternal Wisdom. My today and my tomorrows will be filled with peace.

As my decision yielded to the flow of the Song, the Presence of Goodness was made evident. The Song became an intimate and joyous expression of each moment. New life grew as trust blossomed.

The emptiness of yesterday was replaced by the peacefulness of today. Old fears were melting into a life of happiness created by the rhythm of the Song.

Humility

The rock of humility
is
a safe place to stand in difficult times.

Humility affixes an unbreakable seal
on the lips of arrogance.

Humility makes it possible
for us
to yield into Divine Providence.

The destructive power of envy
can be conquered
by
humility.

Humility is like the butterfly;
the quiet flutter of its wings invites us to follow.

The Song of Source

Days pass in events routine
              beholding the flow of time.
The task at hand is a goal to gain
              the journey to grasp the end.
The quest to strive for me to be
              with power to claim in hand.
On and on the game goes on
              to fill a void in me.
Yet, why so often do I find
              an empty presence as the sign?
In the depths of despair and pain
              a prayer of hope is said.
Through this faith, a power in place
              an open door is shared.
A gentle voice is heard to guide
              with the joy of new beginnings.
The gift is offered for all to gain
              new peace to find a place.
The wind of hope for all to know
              a sail to steer the course.
To walk the path with Love and Grace,
              to share the Song of Source.

Ripples of Sacrifice

Sometimes we must be different to be right.

Weakness and failure are not the end,
but rather
the beginning of opportunity.

The Spirit of Truth
can breathe meaning
into moments of despair.

Realizing the frailty of self
is often the first step
toward seeking divine assistance.

As a good roof gives protection from the storm,
so self-sacrifice and self-discipline
provide a shelter
from the passions and temptations of life.

VIRTUE

Meditation On Virtue

"Finally, brothers, whatever is true,
whatever is honorable,
whatever is just, whatever is pure,
whatever is lovely,
whatever is gracious,
if there is any virtue
and if there is anything worthy of praise,
think about these things."

Philippians 4:8

We, the Gathering

We, the Gathering,
        pray in expectation,
        praise in honor,
        worship in trust.

We, the Gathering,
    listen in patience,
    speak in meekness,
    act in forgiveness.

We, the Gathering,
        live in peace,
        suffer in hope,
        share in joy and sorrow.

We, the Gathering,
    grow through failure,
    recognize with respect,
    accept each other in our
        weaknesses.

We, the Gathering,
        pray in expectation,
        praise in honor,
        worship in trust.

The Mystery

No voice is heard;
> yet the Message is proclaimed.

No vision is seen;
> yet the Eternal Grandeur is beheld.

No feeling is perceived;
> yet the touch of the Divine Presence caresses existence.

No smell is detected;
> yet the Fragrance of Love permeates life.

No taste is savored;
> yet the Sweetness of Peace fills the consciousness.

Ripples of Virtue

Faith
opens a dialogue
with
the Power of Creation.

Honesty is like a cool summer breeze;
it refreshes the spirit.

Wisdom and caring
should
temper the use of power.

Patience helps create the perfect time,
the ideal situation.

The Inheritance

Early one morning we learned the end had arrived. We wanted to experience the familiar touch, but only silence responded. We allowed the pain of the loss to become real. Our sense of security had faded into feelings of weakness and loneliness.

Yesterday, our obligation had been light; today our charge would grow into fullness. A new role was being offered -- the inheritance. We were being called to greater maturity and responsibility in this new reality.

Our bond of Love now sustained us. Our bond of love enabled us to step into tomorrow with shared strength. Drawing upon the gift passed down, we can be an enriched presence of love, a guide to wisdom, and a model of forgiveness.

Give To Me

Give to me your quest for faith;
> I will guide you into knowledge of divine presence.

Give to me your quest for happiness;
> I will offer escape from the enslavement of the world.

Give to me your quest for serenity;
> I will create peace within you.

Give to me your quest for health of mind and body;
> I will heal and protect you.

Give to me your quest for relief from pain;
> I will comfort you throughout all suffering.

Give to me your quest for harmony;
> I will lead you into forgiveness and understanding.

Give to me your quest for prosperity;
> I will open the door to well being.

Give to me your quest for personal esteem;
> I will show you your innate goodness.

Give to me your quest for patience;
> I will teach you to wait in confidence.

The Cup of Wisdom

Hate and love are both generated
from
personal values.

Insecurity is a product of this world;
security is a dimension of God.

We create the prayer;
The Father provides the answer.

Self-worth
is
a reality of God's creation,
not
a struggle to prove personal validity.

Beyond The Veil of Time

The destination is hidden beyond the veil of time;
    yet, the Saving One offers a glimpse of eternal
    bliss.

The security of tomorrow is questionable;
    yet, the Eternal One opens the doors to faith
    and trust.

The haze blurs the light of perception;
    yet, the Divine One offers the rock of security.

Spiritual meaning is clouded in obscurity;
    yet, the Loving One provides understanding.

The mystery is seen in vague shapes and shadows;
    yet, the Knowing One reveals eternal knowledge.

The rocky trail of life can seem fearfully uncertain;
    yet, the Holy One encourages a journey with a
    divine purpose.

Lasting Satisfaction

We often times find ourselves captivated
        by the values and things of this world.

Yet, possessions and control only bring
        limited satisfaction and fleeting fulfillment.

The Truth is in us
        and working to bring us to completion.

A return to the Divine Truth
        offers us a joy and peace that lasts for eternity.

Faith

Faith is:
    an intellectual adherence to a truth,

    a living expression of the elements of belief,

    a mature and a childlike confidence in love.

Faith radiates an attitude of dependence and trust.

Faith can be measured in terms of certainty and commitment.

Faith grows from:
perception	to	understanding;
knowledge	to	practice;
becoming	to	being.

Doing the Word

By Doing the Word, we bring:

Awareness	into	the Fulfillment,
Recognition	into	the Attainment,
Perception	into	the Expression,
Knowledge	into	the Wisdom,
Thought	into	the Action,
Understanding	into	the Response,
Commitment	into	the Accomplishment.

A Flowering Heart

An Image of Eternity
is
seen in the wonders of a beautiful sunrise.

Our Celebration of Life can start each day
recognizing the Divine majesty of creation.

The Fruits of Life are the heavenly gifts
of presence and caring.

The Embrace of Life is evident in the warmth of a smile.

A flowering heart shines
with
the strength of hope and the power of peace.

The Power of Prayer can focus each new morning
upon the quest for goodness.

Pass It On

Don't let it end with you, pass it on:

> the Gift of Love,
> the Word of Truth,
> the Power of Forgiveness,
> the Presence of Peace,
> the Model of Faith,

Don't let it end with you, pass it on.

Ripples of Virtue

The laughter of a child
sings the song of eternity.

As air supports the flight of a bird,
so faith supports the life in the spirit.

Prayer
starts as an idea
and is
expressed as an action.

The biggest part of spirituality is in the doing,
not
in the saying.

True worship is the work of hands.

WISDOM

Meditation of Wisdom

"Turn your ear to wisdom,
inclining your heart to understanding."

Proverbs 2

Let's Get Focused

From: them   to   us,

From: there   to   here,

From: then   to   now,

From: when   to   always,

From: doubt   to   acceptance,

From: distrust   to   conviction.

Ripples of Wisdom

If holiness is valued more than happiness,
then
happiness is guaranteed.

Life offers limited joy if peace is missing.

The magnificence of nature
hints
of a mystery larger than time.

The gentle voice of God
cannot
be heard over the roar of self-concern.

It is Good to Know

The Father   can   only create good.

The Father   can   offer lasting hope.

The Father   will   place judgment.

Divine presence within the moment
offers
the only hope for peace in the world.

Images In Contrast

Shifting sands of uncertainty   or   Solid rock of faith,
Muggy swamp of envy   or   Lush fields of contentment,
Scorching desert of selfishness   or   Quiet waters of service,
Raging storm of suffering   or   Soft touch of healing,

Night of fear   or   Morning of hope,
Winds of pride   or   Gentle breeze of peace,
Tides of doubt   or   Harbor of conviction,
Fire of temptation   or   Hardwood of selfdiscipline,

Clouds of despair   or   Clear skies of confidence,
Raging waters of anger   or   Joyful stream of mercy,
Flood of vanity   or   Calm water of humility.

Mercy and Justice

The Father is not indifferent to evil.

Justice is objective and external.

Mercy is subjective and personal.

It is a contradiction of justice
to disregard evil.

Mercy has precedence over justice.

It is to our advantage
that God's mercy surpasses the call for justice.

Justice will be declared
after kindness has failed.

We impose the Father's judgment upon ourselves.

Boldness Without Kindness

We must be careful not to demonstrate:

Confidence	without	Integrity,
Dominance	without	Compassion,
Loudness	without	Understanding,
Self-assurance	without	Conscience,
Aggressiveness	without	Caring,
Pride	without	Respect,
Boldness	without	Kindness,
Manipulation	without	Sensitivity.

The Balancing Act

Logic   in balance with   Faith,

Emotions   in balance with   Knowledge,

Risk   in balance with   Trust,

Challenge   in balance with   Peace,

Reason   in balance with Wisdom,

Deeds   in balance with   Meditation.

Reality

Forgiveness repairs as Corruption destroys.

Love heals as Evil defiles.

Faith builds as Doubt hinders.

Gentleness caresses as Anger attacks.

Caring reaches as Neglect denies.

Kindness gathers as Hatred separates.

Service offers as Selfishness keeps.

The Mountain

She observed the mountain for many years with passive interest. Its presence drew little attention during the events of her life. It was just there -- hazy in the distance.

As the years came and went, she began to earnestly question the lasting meaning and purpose of her being. Her desire to possess more and more were leading her on a vacant quest. The focus was on the fulfillment of her inward journey. One day she said in hopelessness, "I want more!"

The fog of her mind cleared; and, for the first time, she saw the true dimension of the mountain. With sudden awareness, she beheld the awesome beauty of the mountain. It no longer seemed so far away. Filled with thoughts of wonder, she walked along the path toward the green trees that invited her to the tall mountain. She sensed a compelling force calling her ever nearer to this giant of the horizon.

She climbed the slopes leading to the foothills and beyond. The trail became steeper and the rocks sharper. She was not sure she wanted to keep going; yet, the mystery of the mountain still drew her into enduring hope.

As she continued her trek, she was shocked to hear a distant noise. Her heart raced in anxiety. She first thought to hide; then, she considered that she might be dreaming. The mountain and her journey seemed to swim in the mist of her mind. But no, the sound came again, closer. The sound was real; it revealed another person. She was not alone!

Continued

This person was also on a pilgrimage to reach the top of the mountain. She decided to share the burden of the journey with her new friend. She understood that they needed one another. Together on the way to the summit, they viewed the truth of the mountain.

She knows now that she needed to walk the mountains of life and taste the sweat of wisdom upon her lips. She understands that the journey up the mountain was a gift. She needed to open her life to others. Her inward focus has changed into an outward shower.

Yes, she learned that she is good.
Yes, she learned that we need each other.
Yes, it is a beautiful day to be alive!

Ripples of Wisdom

Forgiveness is a two way street.

Forgiveness
is
both a gift and a responsibility.

Gentleness moves
with
force and assurance.

Faith
is not heard in the voices of people;
but rather
it is seen in their gestures of love and trust.

James Harshfield

Searching ever searching could describe James Harshfield. His curiosity has taken him on a life long journey to discover the core elements of spiritual truths.

Through the guidance of the Spirit of Truth he has been taken:
- from confusion to understanding,
- from complex realities to simple solutions,
- from belief to trust,
- from control to quiet submission,
- from prayers to answers.

His keen insight into life allows him to express spiritual concepts in a unique, gentle, exciting and creative manner. James has bachelor, master, and doctoral degrees in education.